HAVE MORE CENTS

A Young Woman's Guide to Saving Money and Still Doing What You Love

KATIE CHANDLER

© **Copyright 2013 by Empowerment Nation - All rights reserved.**

This publication is designed to provide accurate and authoritative information in regard to the subject matter covered. It is sold with the understanding that the publisher is not engaged in rendering legal, accounting or other professional services. If legal advice or other professional assistance is required, the services of a competent professional person should be sought.

- From a Declaration of Principles jointly adopted by a Committee of the American Bar Association and a Committee of Publishers and Associations.

All rights reserved. No part of this publication may be reproduced or transmitted in any form or by any means, electronic or mechanical, including photocopy, recording, or any information storage or retrieval system, without permission in writing from the publisher.

No responsibility or liability is assumed by the Publisher for any injury, damage or financial loss sustained to persons or property from the use of this information, personal or otherwise, either directly or indirectly. While every effort has been made to ensure reliability and accuracy of the information within, all liability, negligence or otherwise, from any use, misuse or abuse of the operation of any methods, strategies, instructions or ideas contained in the material herein, is the sole responsibility of the reader.

Any copyrights not held by publisher are owned by their respective authors.

All information is generalized, presented for informational purposes only and presented "as is" without warranty or guarantee of any kind.

All trademarks and brands referred to in this book are for illustrative purposes only, are the property of their respective owners and not affiliated with this publication in any way. Any trademarks are being used without permission, and the publication of the trademark is not authorized by, associated with or sponsored by the trademark owner.

EmpowermentNation.com

Table of Contents

Chapter 1: A Brief Introduction to Saving Money ---- 1
    Why Do You Want to Save Money? --- 1
    It Happens Every Day ---- 2
    The Hardest Part: Identifying Wants vs. Needs ---- 4
    Plan Ahead … At Least a Little Bit! --- 7
    Let Your Technology Help You Stay on Budget ---- 8

Chapter 2: Saving Money on Your Most Basic Need: Food ---- 12
    Where You Eat Affects Your Budget --- 12
    How to Save When You Eat Out ---- 13
    How to Save When You Eat In ---- 15
    A Recipe for Money Saving Success --- 18
    Let Your Technology Help You Save on Food ---- 21

Chapter 3: Saving Money on Your Utilities 26
    Little Things Add Up ---- 26
    Taking Advantage of Promotions ---- 29
    Let Your Technology Help You Save on Utilities ---- 31

Chapter 4: Saving Money on Girly Goods and Services ---- 32

How to "Take Down" a CVS ... 32
They Do Exist: Good, Cheap Haircuts ... 35
Save on Nail Care, Too ... 37
Home Spa Extraordinaire: Go DIY for Even More Savings ... 38

Chapter 5: Saving on Miscellaneous Needs ... 40
Getting from A to B: How to Save on Transport ... 40
Under Your Own Roof: How to Save on Goods for Your Home ... 46
Let Technology Help you Save on Decorating ... 48

Chapter 6: How to Save on Your Most Important Want: Wardrobe ... 50
Step One: De-Cluttering ... 50
Step Two: Identifying Your Style Basics ... 54
Step Three: Think "Outfits" ... 56
Where to Shop and Save ... 58
The Bottom Line ... 61
Let Your Technology Help You Save on Clothes and Accessories ... 61

Chapter 7: Save on Entertainment and Lifestyle—Live a Full Life on a Budget ... 65
Watch Movies on the Cheap ... 65

Watch Movies for Even Cheaper
—At Home 67
Staying Fit Without Breaking the Bank 69
Chapter 8: Anyone Can Live on a Budget .. 73
If I Can, You Can 73
What is Saving Money All About 74
Savings Summary: Key Tips
to Remember 75
Good Luck! Now Go Start Saving 80
Wrapping Up: List of Sites and
Apps Mentioned 81

Chapter 1: A Brief Introduction to Saving Money

Why Do You Want to Save Money?

I don't know a single person who is naturally good at saving money. It's something that everyone actively has to work at. I know quite a few "stingy" people, those who refuse to spend money even when it's necessary, but being "stingy" is very different from being good at saving money. To be "good" at saving money, you first need to understand what saving money is all about—for y<u>ou</u>.

Saving money, for me, is about having a little something extra set aside in case of an emergency. Car breaks down? Covered. Spontaneous ski-trip that leads to injury? Covered. For my mom, it's having a little something extra to spend around the holidays, so she can spoil us even in adulthood. What does saving money mean to you? What will it contribute to your life?

Maybe you'll be able to get more sleep, like me, knowing that you're covered in case something unexpected happens. Maybe you want to start stashing money in your mattress because the state of the global economy scares you into hoarding. Maybe you want to be able to take a vacation. Maybe you're saving to buy a house, a car, a boat, a motorcycle, or a hovercraft. It doesn't matter what the reason is, as long as you're committed to it. Saving money is hard. Saving money for a reason you care about and are invested in is a bit easier.

There are dozens of reasons that saving money is hard to do. Humans are social creatures and enjoy contact with other humans. There is no guarantee that the other humans you are spending time with are on the same type of budget that you are. I, for example, have a group of friends who go to get pedicures every week. Unfortunately, I just can't afford to do that. The compromise: I go once a month, and the other three weeks, I give myself a DIY Pedicure in 15 minutes. We'll get to that later.

Would I be able to sacrifice time with my friends and an activity that I enjoy (who doesn't love being pampered?) if I hadn't identified my reasons for saving money? Nope. So figure out your reason for saving money. Stop putting it off until the next paycheck. Saving money is hard, but people do it every day. The successful ones are committed and prepared.

It Happens Every Day

The successful money-savvy people I know are successful because they are prepared. I don't mean that they stockpile coupons in every corner of their home (though my cousin certainly does). I mean that they have a plan. Planning to save money is the only way to actually do it. There are several components to any good money saving plan. The first is your budget.

Sounds simple, right? Make a budget. Everyone does this differently, but there are a few basic steps. To make your budget:
- Know exactly how much money you make every month
- Know exactly how much money you lose every month
- Know exactly how much money you have left over

Your income is likely eaten up every month by expenses that you simply don't have a choice about paying. These are probably things like:
- Rent/mortgage
- Utilities
- Car/transportation
- Insurance
- Debt of any kind (credit card, loans, etc)

If the sum total of these non-negotiable monthly expenses is higher than what you make in a given month, you might want to think about moving. Or getting a roommate. Or taking the bus more. These are the things you can't control —you have to pay for them every month. You can be smart about them, but they must be included in your budget.

The easiest way to make a budget is to use Microsoft Excel. It even does the addition and subtraction for you! Simple as it may seem, writing it down is the first—and most important—step in budgeting. Why? Because it holds you accountable for your spending. So open up Excel right now and start being accountable for your money habits—good and bad. Assign one row in a spreadsheet for every non-negotiable in your life.

The Hardest Part: Identifying Wants vs. Needs

After you've identified the non-negotiable categories in your budget, the hard part begins. In a sense, the more non-negotiable items in your budget, the less you have to identify your own personal wants and needs, because you'll have less room to spend money on them.

On top of the items listed above, there are tons of things for us to spend money on. A comprehensive list of all of them would take up this entire book. From the Home Shopping Channel to the local pharmacy, there are things to buy. Are they useful, necessary things? Sometimes. Do you need them? No—at least, certainly not all of them. I still have a Snuggie warming the back of my closet.

To avoid buying a Snuggie when a simple

sweatshirt/blanket combo will do, you need to establish a hierarchy of your wants. What do you want most? What is most important to you? Past the non-negotiables are the negotiables—the difficulty is that you are negotiating with yourself.

Obviously, you need food. What kind of food? Restaurant quality? Home-cooked? Negotiate with yourself by thinking about your life: how often do you cook vs. go out to eat? Budget accordingly. You also need clothing. What kind of clothing? What kind of wardrobe do you need? Think about your life: do you need more professional clothing, suitable for a work environment? Budget accordingly. Spoiler alert: never fear, these things will be covered later in this book!

Past these negotiables are just pure "wants." They are things that you can live without if you want to be "stingy." On the other hand, they are things that you can incorporate into your life with a little planning and commitment to savings. These are things like:
- Entertainment
- Hobbies
- Lifestyle
- Home décor

I would be lying if I said that I believe you can live a full, enjoyable life without anything from any of these categories. I would also be lying if I said that there was a magic equation that worked for everyone and helped determine which of these categories is most important.

Saving money is not the same for everyone. Perhaps most people have the same non-negotiables, like rent and utilities. Everyone needs a place to live, preferably with electricity. It's the way you view your "wants" that has the power to make or break your budget. I recommend asking yourself these questions to help determine the way you navigate through your "wants" already:

In a typical week:
- How often do you go to a bar?
- How often do you eat out at a restaurant?
- How often do you buy alcohol?
- How often do you order food in/pick-up takeout?
- How often do you workout, and where?

In a typical month:
- How often do you go to the movies?
- How often do you rent movies?
- How often do you go to a concert, play, or sporting event?

The answers to these questions should start to help you identify your habits. I personally did not realize how often I could be found at happy hour in a typical week until I asked myself these questions. At the end of a long work day, when a co-worker asked "Margaritas?" I would almost always say yes. But even one drink adds up when you find yourself saying "Yes!" more than once a week. Even further, one drink may come with snacks or even a full meal. That's money out of your budget without a second thought.

There are ways to save in each of these areas of your life. First, add them to your budget in order of their importance to you. Perhaps after you've answered the questions above, you'll realize that you've been eating out at restaurants a lot—but you enjoy cooking, too. This seems like an obvious accidental gap. You can cut down in one area and bone up in another, and save money at the same time.

When you have a better idea of what you want—and how much you want it, you almost automatically begin to think about how your activities and habits fit into both your life and your budget. This awareness is key to staying on target. You will begin to think twice about margaritas, at the very least!

Plan Ahead ... At Least a Little Bit!

One very difficult thing to do when budgeting is getting into a routine. If you can do it, it will help you immensely. Taking the time to plan out your weekly routine—which days you will cook at home vs. which days you will eat out, whether you want to go out on a Friday night or stay in—will save you money in two ways.

First, it will help keep unexpected expenses from popping up. If you've planned to cook on Tuesdays and taken the chicken out of the freezer, for example, you're less likely to ditch those plans for dinner out at a restaurant. It's not that you have to do the same thing every week—switch it up as often as you like. The point is to be cognizant of your day, week, or month enough to plan ahead. Life is full of enough unexpected expenses. If you are expecting some of them, saving money will be much easier.

Second, there are basically "deals" for every day of the week. What if, all along, you were eating out on random weeknights when Wednesday nights offered buy-one-get-one entrees? Why wait until Friday to see a movie if your theater has "Bargain Tuesday?" Planning ahead, even just a little, can keep money in your pocket.

Let Your Technology Help You Stay on Budget

Finally, possibly the most important thing you can learn about living frugally and saving money is that you don't have to do it alone. I don't mean that you need to get all your friends to do it too or that you need tangible support from other people. The best and easiest way to save money is to let your technology help you.

Of course, this is easier if you have a

smartphone, because you always have the power of savings in your hand wherever you go. However, all you really need is a computer, and the Internet can start helping you to save money right away.

There are literally hundreds of websites that can help you save money in various areas of your life. There are also dozens of apps for smartphones that do the same. Although it's not a bad idea to clip coupons every week, the era of couponing in the traditional sense is over. Let your coupons, offers, sale updates, weekly deals, promotions, and rewards come right to your e-mail inbox.

This book will help you get on—and stay on—a budget. It will also help you find and navigate the technology that will make it easy to do so. The first chapter of this book has been about the beginnings of budgeting—where and how to start actually making a budget. After you've made your Excel spreadsheet of wonder, you should check out the following apps and websites that will make budgeting and staying on a budget that much easier.

- Mint.com
  Mint.com will literally do the work for you. It is a great tool, especially in the first month of budgeting, to help you see exactly where you're on budget and where you're off. First, you link your

banking information to Mint.com—it's free, and takes about three minutes to sign up. It will tell you what categories you spend the most money in, as often as you like—bi-weekly, monthly, etc. It will also allow you to set savings goals and then offers tips and next steps for achieving those goals. Finally, there's a mobile app as well, which makes it even easier to keep track of your finances on the go.

- Rudder.com
  Rudder.com is quite like Mint.com in that it allows all of your finances to be viewed in one place. However, it goes a step further than Mint.com because it's focused on the future and not the past. Where Mint.com's strength is showing you what you have been spending, Rudder.com shows you what you have left to spend in the future, while still paying your bills. It also has a mobile app for easy money management on the move.

- Geezeo.com
  Geezeo offers the same functionality that Mint.com does, too, but it puts a bit of a different spin on it. While you can use it to manage your money, you also have the

opportunity to partake in a sort of online community related to your financial goals. This is great for the socializing money savvy among us—it allows you to learn from other people who have the same money concerns, problems, and questions as you. Who knows what the average individual trying to save money is going through? Now, you can!

Chapter 2: Saving Money on Your Most Basic Need: Food

Where You Eat Affects Your Budget

It's no surprise that where you eat, when you eat, and how often you eat can be a huge factor in your budget and in your life in general. The first step in saving money on food, really, is eating out less. Everyone says it, all the time, and we all know it's true: restaurants are more expensive than cooking at home. The problems are: cooking takes time, energy, and planning. Cooking also involves grocery shopping, which takes time, energy, and planning. Maybe you hate cooking. Maybe you're just not good at it. I won't tell you that the only way you can save money is by cooking for yourself or your family, though it does help. Instead, I'll show you some easy ways to save money eating both out and in—and breaking down the "eating in" category into useful and easy to follow chunks.

I will say, though, that if you buy coffee every morning, you are wasting money. Even if you forego the very expensive Starbucks for the less expensive Dunkin' Donuts or even 7-Eleven, you could still be saving that money. The first move I made toward trying to save money was to start making my coffee at home, and taking it with me in a travel mug. I now save $1.79 per day, which is roughly $40.00 a month, just by setting my coffee maker to start brewing in the morning. Take a small, easy, first step and start making your own coffee today. You may even discover that you like it better!

How to Save When You Eat Out

So, you hate cooking. Or your significant other or child hates your cooking. At least once per week, you eat in a restaurant, order in, or take out. It really is harder to save money if you do this on a more regular basis, but it can be done! If eating in a restaurant is ranked highly among your negotiables, go for it. Just try a few of these tips and ideas to make it cheaper.

First of all, there are many restaurants that have daily, weekly, or monthly deals, as I mentioned earlier. Many of these restaurants are chain restaurants, which means you're likely to find one nearby. The menu at most chain restaurants is generally broad enough to have something for everyone.

Take Carrabba's, for example. Carrabba's has a new special for every season. At one point, the seasonal deal at Carrabba's was free seconds on pasta entrees. Just buy one pasta dish, with a side salad or soup, for $13.00. Then get seconds for free. Take home an entire meal. Carrabba's also had (and may still have) "Wine Wednesday"—all of their sangrias were half price, at $5.00 per glass.

Applebee's, too, has had deals like "Pick-n-Pair" lunches for under $10 and 2 for $20 deals on appetizers and entrees—so that two people can enjoy a meal for $20.00. There are many restaurants where kids eat for free on certain days of the week: Denny's, Buffalo Wild Wings, and CiCi's Pizza, just to name a few.

Most chain restaurants also have some kind of rewards card. Carrabba's, for example, has "Amici Club." It's free to join and will e-mail you coupons, special offers, and updates about the seasonal special. Look into your options before you head out to eat at one of the many chain restaurants in your area.

If eating at a big, flashy chain restaurant isn't your style (believe me, it's not mine either), there are still ways to save. The first is to go for lunch instead of dinner. Lunch deals tend to be much cheaper than dinner and often include different options on a prix-fix menu.

If lunch isn't an option for you, there are tons of ways you can save at any meal, even dinner. The first is simple: eat something before you go. If you eat a snack before you head to the restaurant, even just an apple, you're less likely to over-order and get carried away by hunger pangs.

If you want to enjoy something delicious

without breaking the bank, you can also order appetizers as your meal. Yes, the portions are obviously smaller, but the dishes are also cheaper. If you've scarfed down your apple prior to hitting the restaurant, appetizers may do just fine for you. If you've skipped the pre-restaurant snack, think about sharing food. Splitting an entrée is a great way to save money, especially because most restaurant portions are easily big enough for two.

It should go without saying, but a very easy way to save money when eating out is to avoid drinking. Tap water is free, while cocktails can be upwards of $10.00 in some places. Though it might be more enjoyable to have a drink with your meal, if you need to cut corners somewhere, cut the booze. You went out to eat, after all, not to drink!

How to Save When You Eat In

If you tend to eat in more often than out, congratulations! You are probably already saving money compared to others and certainly compared to me. However, there are ways to save even more when you eat in and cook for yourself or your family.

First, plan your meals. It may seem simple, but many people don't do it. I myself didn't do it and would find myself at the grocery store after work, wandering around looking for ingredients for a hypothetical meal I hadn't planned. Yes, I would argue this is better than finding myself in a restaurant for dinner, but I also believe that unplanned grocery store adventures can be a huge waste of money.

Take twenty to thirty minutes out of your week to think about what to cook on what days. You don't have to be Wolfgang Puck to do this. Start with something easy: protein. Where will the protein in your meal come from? Then move through the major food groups. Repeat for all the days of the week that you can commit to cooking. If you can't donate twenty to thirty minutes to making a detailed plan, make a commitment to think about meal-planning at another time of your day: while driving, folding laundry, or cleaning the bathroom.

If you have a basic idea of a week's meals, you have a basic idea of what to get at the grocery store. Write this down. Just like writing down all of your expenses makes you more accountable for them, writing down your grocery needs helps you stick to them.

When you plan your meals ahead, you can buy more in bulk and save. Most grocery stores sell meat and frozen food items in large quantities for less money. For example, ShopRite sells individually wrapped chicken breasts in sheets (literally, perforated sheets) of 10-20. I buy them at the beginning of the month, pop them in the freezer, and defrost as needed.

The same can be done with vegetables. Buying veggies and freezing them right away still preserves the nutritional value (thanks, mom, for that tip!) but also ensures that they don't go bad if you can't use them all right away. However, if you buy your vegetables in the grocery store, I recommend only buying what you need for a given week. If you want to save even more money on produce, look for your local farmer's market, produce junction, or farm stand. Not only can you usually haggle for better prices at these places, you get farm-fresh produce for less money.

Most farmer's markets and produce junctions only accept cash. This is actually better for those on a budget—whereas it's easy to swipe your credit or debit card and not know your balance until you check it, if you know you left the house with $20.00 in your wallet and came home with $0, you are automatically aware of how much you spent.

Every other Sunday, I go to my town's "produce junction." It's open year-round, only takes cash, and has a better variety of produce than my local grocery store. I usually spend somewhere between $10.00-$12.00 and walk out with enough produce to last at least two weeks. What I don't use right away (I can't eat two pounds of broccoli in one week!) I freeze for later. That way, I always have some frozen vegetables on hand in case I haven't been able to plan ahead that week to have fresh ones on hand.

Another way to have great, fresh veggies on hand at all times is to start a garden. Not only do you get fresh produce, you also get a fun hobby. If space is an issue, try a container garden on your balcony or windowsill. Even just growing herbs is helpful, fun, fragrant, and a money-saver!

A Recipe for Money Saving Success

It is also much easier to plan your meals if you follow recipes—family recipes, cookbook recipes, or recipes you find on the Internet. Although I frequently use websites like allrecipes.com, which have great meal ideas, my favorite website for recipes is a blog called budgetbytes.blogspot.com.

This website is literally the perfect way to save money on food. Every recipe is explained thoroughly, so even those who aren't Chef Boyardee can follow. More importantly, every recipe is also broken down by how many people it serves and by much each ingredient costs.

Take this example recipe from Budget Bytes for "Zesty Tomato and Artichoke Pasta." The whole recipe costs only $5.14, and serves 4. That breaks down to a cost of $1.29 per serving!

INGREDIENTS		COST
1 recipe	Sun Dried Tomato Sauce	$1.17
8 oz.	bow tie pasta	$0.55
3 cups	fresh spinach	$0.50
1 (13 oz.) can	artichoke hearts	$2.50
1/4 cup	grated parmesan (optional)	$0.42
TOTAL		**$5.14**

STEP 1: Bring a large pot of water to a rolling boil over high heat. When it reaches a boil, add the pasta and continue to let it boil for 7-10 minutes, or until the pasta is tender. Drain the cooked pasta in a colander.

STEP 2: While waiting for the pasta to cook, prepare the Sun Dried Tomato Sauce.

INGREDIENTS		COST
1/3 cup	olive oil	$0.64
1 clove	garlic, minced	$0.08
1/2 tsp	dried oregano	$0.03
1/2 tsp	dried basil	$0.03
1/4 tsp	dried thyme	$0.02
1/4 tsp	dried rosemary	$0.02

a pinch	crushed red pepper	$0.02
10-15 cranks	freshly cracked pepper	$0.02
1/2 tsp	salt	$0.02
3 oz.	tomato paste	$0.27
1/2 tsp	honey	$0.02
TOTAL		**$1.17**

SAUCE STEP 1: Add the olive oil, garlic, basil, oregano, thyme, rosemary, crushed red pepper, salt, and some freshly cracked pepper to a small skillet. Stir and heat the mixture over low heat for about 3-5 minutes. It's okay if it sizzles slightly, but you don't want it to get hot enough that the herbs burn.

SAUCE STEP 2: Add the tomato paste and honey. Allow it to heat through as you stir. It will not form a smooth sauce. Continue to stir and heat over low for about 5 minutes or until you notice the tomato paste has darkened slightly. Either use immediately or refrigerate until ready to use!

Once the sauce is finished, add the fresh spinach, stir, and cook it over low until the spinach wilts (1-2 min.). Drain the artichoke hearts, roughly chop them, and then add them to the skillet with the tomato sauce and spinach.

STEP 3: Once the pasta is cooked and drained, add it to the skillet with the sauce, and stir until everything is coated and combined. Serve hot with a sprinkle of Parmesan cheese over top if desired.

If you need to start saving money on food, but you still want to eat well—not to mention healthy—Budget Bytes is a great resource. There is something for everyone—it has vegetarian and vegan options, as well as gluten-free ideas. It also has links to other food and recipe blogs, so if you don't find what you are looking for at Budget Bytes, you can use it as a starting point and look around elsewhere.

Let Your Technology Help You Save on Food

Budget Bytes isn't the only way to use technology to help you save money on good eating. There are hundreds of websites and apps to help you do so too. Check out the following sites and apps that help you save money when you dine out:

- Restaurants.com
  Restaurants.com is great because it allows you to put in your zip code for local deals near you. Once you put your zip code in, you can look at a list of restaurants near you that are selling gift

cards. These gift cards are not full price—you can get a gift card worth $50.00 for only $25.00. Sometimes the gift cards even go on sale, so you can get a great deal and pay $5.00 for $25.00 worth of food. The downside is that there is no mobile app, so you have to keep checking back to get the best deals.

- Groupon.com

  Signing up for Groupon can potentially save you money in various areas of your life, and we'll cover some of them later. However, Groupon offers lots of restaurant deals. Just sign up using your e-mail address and get deals daily. Most of the restaurant deals on Groupon are discounts from 30% to 75%. You simply buy the Groupon off the site, and show it at the restaurant—easy, of course, because they have a mobile app.

- Scoutmob

  Scoutmob is an app that has restaurant deals in many major US cities. It probably isn't very effective for you if you live out in the Burbs, but depending on how often you venture into a large city, you have the option to save! It offers approximately $20-$25 off of your check. The best part? When the check comes, you just pull up the app on your phone and show it to your server.

- ChowHound.com
  ChowHound is a great site, but it doesn't OFFER any deals. It's great because it's just a bunch of people who love food, writing about the food that they love and where to get it cheaply. You can browse through different topics on the site—where to get cheap Chinese food in this city, what restaurants are BYOB in that city—and discover some hidden gems and cheap eats!

There are also tons of apps and sites that help you save money on eating in. The best way to save money eating in, obviously, is to save money on groceries. The old-fashioned way is to clip coupons, which my parents still do every Sunday. The cool, up-to-the-minute way to do it is to utilize the power of technology! Check out these apps and websites that help you save on groceries and eating in:

- CouponSherpa
  CouponSherpa is a mobile app, and also has a website. It's got more coupons in one place than your average mail circular, and you don't even have to print or cut to use them. Just scan them on your phone!

- GroceryIQ

  GroceryIQ is more specifically tailored to grocery shopping than CouponSherpa. Like CouponSherpa, it does have coupons embedded in the app. It also allows you to track the items you buy often to a type of "favorites" section, which saves you time later. You can actually use it to make a grocery list and stick to it, and if you want to update your list on the website, it will automatically sync with your mobile app.

- Coupons.com

  Sounds obvious, doesn't it? Not nearly enough people take advantage of the great grocery coupons on coupons.com. The site is organized into categories for easy searching (food, healthcare, cleaning, etc). As the tagline of the website says "Just click, print, and save!" It's true—I've used coupons from coupons.com to save on everything from laundry detergent to cereal!

These little grocery hacks are just three of many out there. The most important thing to remember, whether you're eating in or dining out, is to use your technology to your advantage! Get on the Internet and check to see if that restaurant you've been dying to check out has any deals or specials going on. Use the free apps you've downloaded to get things at the grocery store for less! It doesn't take much; with just a little planning, you can start saving while still eating great.

Chapter 3: Saving Money on Your Utilities

Little Things Add Up

Anyone who is even mildly environmentally conscious knows to turn off the lights when leaving a room. You'd be surprised, though, the impact that habit can have on your utility bill each month. In fact, there are tons of little ways to keep your electric bill down. Some of them require sacrifice, but some require only planning.

In addition to turning the lights off when you leave, make sure that all other appliances are off as well. Remember to turn off your cable box—something I always forget about. Of course, now that we've got fancy TV options like DVR, no one wants to miss a chance to record a show. You can do this and still turn your cable box off—just set it on a timer.

In fact, you can set any electrical appliance to shut off on a timer. Timers themselves are relatively inexpensive, and can be found at Lowes, Home Depot, or any hardware store.

Washing machines and dish washers contribute to your electricity bill more than you think. This is because both of these appliances require hot water to do a proper cleaning job. Unfortunately, that water also first needs to be heated—which is about 80% of the energy that your washing machine and dishwasher use.

First, to cut costs when washing clothing simply wash your clothes using cold water. It saves a bit of money, and it also improves the lifetime of your clothing—less fading and shrinking happen in cold water. Some people argue that washing your clothing in hot water is better for sanitation—that hot water kills germs. No one argues with this! However, most clothing is not dirty enough to warrant using hot water. I wouldn't call any of my t-shirts unsanitary, and I wash them in cold water.

Second, think about the time you wash your clothing. Surprisingly, most power companies have a little well-kept secret: there are "peak" electricity usage times. These times vary depending on your provider, but "peak" times for most electricity and energy companies are during the day. Check with your provider (this may require calling—mine did) to see which hours are cheapest—and run your washer, dryer, and dishwasher then.

Since 80% of the energy your dishwasher uses involves heating the water, and you actually do need hot water to wash the dishes, the same trick won't work here. The obvious tips are to run the dishwasher only when it is full, rinse your dishes before washing, and avoid putting bigger items like pots and pans in the dishwasher. A not-so-obvious tip is to take a hard look at your dishwasher to see if it has a "heated dry" setting. If your dishwasher does have this setting (and most do), de-select it. There's no reason to heat your dishes until they are dry! Sure, it's annoying to open the dishwasher and have to do a bit of drying by hand before putting the dishes away. If you commit to this though, the energy your dishwasher uses per load can decrease up to 15%, according to the technician who installed my dishwasher. Don't choose the longest cycle for your dishes, either—if you rinse them before putting them in, the shortest setting will clean everything just as well.

Something my mom has been telling me since before I left for college is that you can save big if you unplug your appliances before leaving the house. I didn't believe her. I thought that the nuisance of having to run around and unplug everything would be more annoying than cost effective. I was wrong!

My electricity bill has decreased by $15 every month since I started unplugging appliances around the house. Now, I unplug everything after I've used it—the coffee pot, the toaster—everything in the kitchen. Things like TVs, DVD players, and cable boxes are more difficult. However, batching these electronics near one another (as they naturally would be in any home) makes it easy to use power strips. Plug everything into a power strip, and unplug the power strip. Voila: extra money every month.

Investing in CFL light bulbs can save money, too. According to Home Depot they use up to 75% less energy. Making a small investment now can save money in the long run. The same goes for "smart" chargers—they shut off when an electronic device is fully charged. You may have to spend a bit of money to save money over time, but it's worth it. Older electronics use more electricity than newer ones in a lot of cases. Replacing all of my power strips with newer, "smart" ones has helped me to cut energy costs too.

Finally, use your thermostat! Everyone likes to be comfortable, that's a given. If you add even a few degrees by turning down the AC or the heat, you can save a bit extra every month. According to energysavers.gov, you can save 1% for every degree change if that degree change lasts for eight hours or more.

Taking Advantage of Promotions

Cable companies are full of hidden tips and tricks for saving money. Cable bills can be expensive, especially if you enjoy having a variety of options. However, cable can also end up as an unnecessary expense, because, thanks to online sources like Netflix and Hulu, you can watch almost anything over the Internet. The first step in cutting costs related to cable is to look at your bill. How many of those channels are you actually watching? How many of the shows you watch can be found in other places?

Once you've established which channels you want to keep, you can talk to your cable company about deals. Sometimes it's as easy as getting a customer service representative on the phone. Here are some things to talk to your cable provider about:

- Ask about bundling some "premium" channels with your regular package (Showtime, HBO, etc). Doing this resulted in my cable company giving me 6 months free HBO!

- Ask about bundling your cable and internet. There's no reason not to. Almost every provider does this now. And when you do it, go to BestBuy and buy your own router—there's no reason to pay a fee every month to rent a router from your cable and Internet provider!

- Some cable companies offer promotions for signing on. In many cases, these offer a lower intro rate for new customers for a certain number of months. For example, our cable and Internet provider offered the first six months of service at a cheaper promotional rate. Look into these when you're selecting a cable company.

Let Your Technology Help You Save on Utilities

Although there aren't exactly apps to download to help you save money on your utilities, there's one website that can really help you cut costs. This amazing website is Billshrink.com. You can use it to compare providers for different services—cell phone plans, cable, Internet—and choose the competitive price. All you do is put in your zip code and see the local offers. It also helps you navigate which credit cards are best, and all you need to do is put in your average credit card spending.

Although technology is extremely helpful in most areas of money-saving, I think that with regard to cable, Internet, and cell phone savings, there is no substitute for getting in touch with a customer service representative on the phone. It really doesn't ever hurt to ask!

Chapter 4: Saving Money on Girly Goods and Services

How to "Take Down" a CVS

When I first moved out on my own, my cousin (the expert coupon clipper mentioned earlier) told me that the easiest way to save money on tons of basic needs was to "take down CVS." That is her phrase, not mine, but it's a fairly accurate representation of the possible savings when this is done right.

There are several steps to understanding this process. I can only hope that if I explain it here as it was explained to me, you will also leave CVS with seven items and one dollar back in your pocket. Yup! That is right. I made money using this process. Being a woman is expensive—and most of the things I want and need at CVS are beauty products. There are always great deals to be found in the beauty section, but do not neglect the cleaning supply or even food sections when using this "take down" strategy.

The first step is to go to CVS and get an ExtraCare Rewards Card. You can do this online via the CVS website or right in store. The benefit to doing it in-store, of course, is that you get the card right away and begin saving immediately!

The next step is to register your card online at CVS.com.

This rewards card will do a lot of things for you automatically, including:

- Give you "bucks" at the end of every quarter. CVS will give you 2% of your spending every quarter right back to you in the form of ExtraCare Bucks. These "Bucks" print at the end of your receipt. They are literally free money to use at CVS on almost anything. There are restrictions, but they are rare.

- Give you $1 in "Bucks" for every two prescriptions you fill.

- When CVS lists a sale item, that sale item sometimes comes with "Bucks"—for example, these advertisements usually say something like "conditioner, $3.99 with $2.00 ExtraCare Bucks. Instead of printing only at the end of every quarter, these "bucks" print immediately when you make the purchase.

Be careful, because this free money expires! It usually doesn't expire for at least 30 days after it's issued, so you do have time.

The easiest way to start saving is to pick up the CVS "circular" every week and use it in combination with your rewards card. The ads are put out every Sunday. You can get them if you have a newspaper delivery—they're in your Sunday paper. What, you haven't noticed them yet?! If you don't have a paper delivered or regularly buy a Sunday paper, you can get them from your local CVS. You know those stands you always ignore when you walk into a CVS? They're full of savings!

These circulars have coupons, which we already understand are good (specifically, they are good if they are an item you would already be buying!). They also have general advertisements indicating what items in the store have lower prices for the week. These are great to look through just to understand the potential savings without your rewards card. However, these circulars also have specific deals for ExtraCare Rewards members. The ad tells you what you pay and how many "Bucks" you get back. These deals are usually marked in yellow and have some fine print at the bottom, while other ads will just say the price with a picture of the item.

Here's the big deal. Are you ready? You are about to learn how to make your "bucks" save you even more money. By using your rewards card in combination with coupons and the circulars, you can save money and get money back. You can get even more money back, however, by *spending your ExtraCare Bucks on items that get you more ExtraCare Bucks.*

Example: At the end of the quarter, I had $7.00 in ExtraCare Bucks. I used them to buy items that ended up giving me $5.00 MORE in ExtraCare Bucks, by looking in the circular to see what the smart purchases would be. What does this mean? Free money for buying things at CVS. Start taking advantage of this system now, and thank my cousin for her expertise.

They Do Exist: Good, Cheap Haircuts

It's hard to imagine getting a good haircut for a low price. It's especially hard to imagine sacrificing quality on something like a haircut, because it drastically changes your look. Never fear: it is possible to get a cheap haircut without sacrificing quality.

First, you don't need to go to a boutique salon for quality hair care. If you have a Hair Cuttery, Super Cuts, or Great Clips near you, you can get a good hair cut for a low price. As with any good hair cut experience, the number one most important thing is to develop a relationship with your stylist. This can be done anywhere—a small salon or a chain salon. Especially if you're looking for hair color, a chain salon can do all-over color for significantly less than a private salon. Though I used to be dubious of the quick and cheap cuts at chain salons, I recently went to a Hair Cuttery in my hometown. I received a free consultation about my hair. It included what products to use as well as what haircuts would look best with the shape of my face. The haircut itself included a wash with high-end shampoo and conditioner. I paid $23.00 and got to know my stylist, Dana. All of my details were put into their computer system, and I was entered into a rewards program.

It is equally possible to get an affordable haircut at a salon, if you don't have much salon loyalty. Most salons offer promotions to get new customers in the door—some offer up to 50% off of one service for a new customer. If you don't love your stylist, or you're willing to try someone new for a better price, shop around at salons you haven't been to. New salons offer promotions too, to build a customer base. Look in your local newspaper and circulars for new salons opening up and see what the offers are. Even just calling a local salon to make an appointment can result in a cheaper 'do. Ask when you schedule if the salon has a junior stylist or someone in training, and see what possible reduced prices they offer for scheduling an appointment with one.

Finally, the best haircut tip I've ever been given actually resulted in a free haircut! Many beauty schools offer free haircuts in order to help train their stylists. Almost all beauty schools offer this—meaning even brand name salons, like Aveda, have their own beauty schools and are giving away haircuts for free. Be careful—usually, giddy on the high of a free, new look, I'm tempted to buy tons of hair products right from the salon—don't do this! The prices are higher for the same or similar products in the salon than they are in stores like Target or Ulta.

Save on Nail Care, Too

I used to wait until the day of an event to get my nails done, because it seemed logical: getting your nails done at the last minute means they won't have time to chip or break before the event! Unfortunately, most events worthy of a manicure occur on the weekends—when nail prices are usually 25% higher.

First of all, getting a manicure with a pedicure usually saves a couple bucks. Getting them separately, at different times, certainly doesn't save you anything. Additionally, and more importantly, most nail salons offer a cheaper price for a manicure-pedicure combo on Monday, Tuesday, and Wednesday. For example, my local nail salon charges $15.00 for a manicure. Monday through Wednesday they charge $17 for a manicure-pedicure combo. It's a big savings if girly salon time is something you enjoy, as I do.

You can also save money on nails by getting them done less often, as seems obvious. Of course, the quality of a manicure deteriorates over time. The trick to keeping our nails looking constantly beautiful, ladies, is to do touch ups ourselves! It seems simple—but so many people do not do it. Why? The colors in the nail salon are attractive and bright, and there is so much variety. Even I am likely to get distracted by all of the pinks and oranges. However, I don't own any of those colors myself, so if my nails chip, I can't touch them up. I don't choose them. Now, I always choose a color that I know I have at home (or bring it myself—and once I got $1 off for doing so!) so I can keep my nails looking great for longer.

Home Spa Extraordinaire: Go DIY for Even More Savings

An even easier way to save money, of course, is to do all of these things at home. I have had home haircut and hair color experiences with varying degrees of success. If you have a friend or family member willing to do either, it's worth a try, right?

While I am no expert at DIY haircuts and hair color, I am an expert at DIY nail care. This is thanks in large part to my mom, who taught me long ago that there's nothing you can't do at home that gets done in a salon!

Buy all the necessities: polish, top and bottom coat (or a combo, from Essie, for $6 at any pharmacy), clippers, a cuticle cutter, and cotton swabs. Investing in these items may cost you anywhere from $15-$30, but if you stay true to the DIY Mani-Pedi, you can save at least that much in a two month period.

Chapter 5: Saving on Miscellaneous Needs

Getting from A to B: How to Save on Transport

As I write this, I am on a bus. Personally, I am on a MegaBus, cruising through the great state of Pennsylvania. I bought this ticket yesterday for $29, one way from Philadelphia to Pittsburgh. Had I bought the ticket seven days prior, I would have paid as little as $8!

There are multiple budget bus options for the adventurous traveler—MegaBus has stops in hundreds of cities all over the United States. Several smaller bus companies populate the northeastern U.S. with dozens of trips daily between popular cities such as New York and Washington, D.C.

Bus travel is not for the faint of heart—this much I know. However, bus travel has an outdated reputation in American society. It's a bit better than you may have heard. For starters, MegaBus and other smaller coach bus companies offer complimentary wireless internet on the bus. Most buses now are double-decker. The stops are convenient—near a train station or transit hub in most major cities. The times are even more convenient, as there are generally many trips on any given day. Finally, every time I've taken a MegaBus trip, I've had not just a seat, but an entire row to myself. I have never seen a MegaBus full, even when I traveled from New York City to Washington D.C. on July 3. Buses are a best kept secret.

In an effort to gauge how much I was going to save by taking the bus for this trip, I calculated what driving would cost me. Using www.gasbuddy.com/trip, I calculated the cost of gas for the trip based on average prices. Then I added the cost of tolls. Finally, I thought about my car, and what the trip would do to it. It's easy to hop in the car and head to wherever you want to go, but taking a little time to consider your options could save you tons.

The mileage from Philadelphia to Pittsburgh is roughly:

At approximately $3.75 per gallon, with a car that gets about 30 miles to the gallon highway, I would have paid $64.00 just for gas alone—one way. Add to that all of the tolls, for a total of $208.00 and my comfy Megabus seat is looking great for $29.

The cost of gas is something that I constantly hear people talking about. Casual chit-chat or small talk that used to be about the weather has transitioned into a quick exchange about gas prices. It is a sad fact of American life: getting around is getting more expensive.

However, even if you absolutely refuse to take the bus, you can save a bit getting around in your own car.

The first trick to not spending tons of money on gas is just three small words: regularly scheduled maintenance. This is common sense, right? If your car is regularly maintained, whether that involves an oil change or a tire pressure check, it will run better. If it runs better, it will get better mileage. Better mileage means less money on gas.

Take this advice one step further and learn how to do an oil change at home here: www.edumunds.com. The "Car Maintenance" section breaks the process down into steps. You will save even more, and although there is a bit of a learning curve, it's easy. If I can do it, you can do it! If you don't feel comfortable or skilled enough to change your own oil, at the very least you can be sure to check the pressure of your tires often and to put air in them when necessary. This, too, is part of regularly scheduled maintenance. Even my owner's manual says that keeping tires full improves the car's mileage.

Next, do not drive like a maniac. The harder you slam on the breaks, the more gas you use. Just the same, the faster you accelerate, the more gas you use. Chill out, save money. It's that simple. Of course, there are times when perfectly smooth driving is impossible to achieve. Hoping this is a result of traffic and not uncontrollable road rage, I will advise you to simply leave a little earlier to get where you're going. Try listening to something soothing while you drive. Whatever you need to do to stop driving like a maniac will be worth it—one tank of gas will last a lot longer than it used to!

Maybe it's just not possible for you to stop driving like Michael Schumacher, and that's fine. In that case, pay attention to your fill-up habits more than your driving habits. What kind of fueler are you? Do you wait until your gas light comes on to fill up? Do you fill up on a more regular schedule? Everyone is different. I have picked up a co-worker on the side of the road because she ran out of gas en route to work. I personally get gas only on Wednesdays. I never let my car dip below a quarter of a tank. Why, you ask? Simple—I like to save money.

Your fill-up habits don't have to mirror mine—there is really just one simple rule to follow: never fill up your gas tank over the weekend. Unless there is an emergency of some kind, avoid the gas station at all costs from Thursday morning until Sunday night. Gas stations increase their prices towards the end of the week in anticipation of weekend travel. So, if you are not traveling for the weekend, save the extra $.03 or $.05 per gallon by filling up Monday through Wednesday.

I try to keep my car at least one quarter full at any given time for two reasons. The first is most important to me personally: I don't like emergencies. The second is important for my car: according to my mechanic, a car's engine runs better that way. As he put it, "it's better when it's not pulling up all the gross stuff sitting in the bottom of the gas tank." Having never seen the inside of a gas tank, I don't know what that means exactly.

Additionally: use your air conditioning sparingly. Air conditioning, according to fueleconomy.gov, uses up to 8% of the fuel that you put into your car. While cruising around town, just open your windows. The drag from having the windows open is still more efficient on fuel than running the AC at that speed. Everyone likes to be comfortable—but putting the vents on or opening your windows instead of using the AC will cut down on fuel costs over time.

As you can tell, saving money on gas is really just a matter of common sense. Just like you would with any other purchase, make sure that you shop around for the best deals. There's a great website (and mobile app!) that can help with this. Gasbuddy.com requires only your zip code or location and it will find the cheapest gas station in your area. I like using this website because it's helpful, but also because they did something charitable that I respect: just after hurricane Sandy, they identified gas stations in the affected areas that still had gas left. They also listed when a gas station was getting a shipment, and how long the gas lines were at certain stations. Way to go, gasbuddy.com. It's the little things that count.

Further reason for you to start doing all of these things (or any combination of them) is a testimonial from my own life. I started using these tips in my own life, and I've saved about $40.00 in the course of three months. Not too shabby for some simple changes!

To sum up, you can save money on gas if you:

- Fill your tank up *full*. Putting $10.00 in at a time doesn't save you any money—you have to use gas to go to the gas station more often.
- Keep your driving as smooth as possible.
- Take care of your car in every way you can.
- Shop around for gas prices.

Seems pretty simple, right? It is! You can also use some handy websites to help you. They are:

- Fueleconomy.gov
  This website will tell you everything you need to know about gas: where to get it, how to get it, how to save, and more.

- Gasbuddy.com

As mentioned earlier, this website will help you find the cheapest gas in your area, calculate the cost and mileage of a trip, and provides little tips and tricks for filling up on the cheap.

- Wikihow.com/save-money-on-gas
  If you are looking for more detail about the ways to save money on gas listed above, this may be the website for you. It explains 25 ways to save money on gas, some of which are not very relevant (buy a new car, for example) but some of which are helpful!

Under Your Own Roof: How to Save on Goods for Your Home

Everyone wants to have a beautiful home. Your home is where you spend most of your time, and it should be a reflection of you. It should also make you feel comfortable. Unfortunately, advertising capitalizes on this ideal. This sometimes results in the idea that in order to build a beautiful home, you have to spend a lot of money. This tendency is furthered by a lack of time. It takes time to pick pieces and beautiful things to fill your home. Since no one wants to be living on milk crates, the tendency is just to *buy*.

Some simple tips for savings on furniture

and décor:

- Don't just buy—know what you need. Buy only those things.
- Be nice to the salesperson. I believe this is just the proper thing to do in life in general, but I also did get a free lamp and a discount on a chair when I was really extra nice.
- Look for sales—the right ones. Some furniture sales are just gimmicks. Look for floor samples, closeout sales, and clearance sales. Every year Macy's has a clearance rug event, for example. These are the sales that really *are* going to save you money, not just get you in the door and trick you.
- Shop at clearance and outlet centers. These places do probably sell some damaged furniture, but they also just sell cast offs that haven't been bought yet. These are also often great places to find furniture because they usually have some one-of-a-kind stuff that you won't find if you just hop into Ethan Allen.
- Buy used furniture. While I wouldn't recommend buying a used mattress, what's wrong with buying a used kitchen table? Consignment shops, estate sales, and auctions are great places to get cheap furniture.

Understandably, not everyone has time to DIY everything. However, for savings in home décor, there's no better way to keep money in your pocket than making things yourself. I recommend using sites like Pinterest.com to organize your décor ideas. There are tons of DIY ideas with images that you can "pin" electronically to different "boards." For example, I have a "bathroom" board with cute decorating ideas. One of them is a DIY earring stand, which I made myself for under $5.00 with a picture frame, wire mesh, and super glue.

Let Technology Help you Save on Decorating

There are some good apps and sites that can help you save money when decorating.

- Onekingslane.com
  Register for this website and get daily email deals on beautiful designer goods for your home. The deals are on everything from throw pillows to silverware.

- DealDecor.com
  This site advertises itself as "a smarter way to shop for furniture" and it really is. It offers great deals on everything you could ever need for your home, and

coupons on top of it. Generally, you can find deals for up to 70% off!

- YipIt.com
    This site is not exclusively for home décor, but that is how it started. It updates you on *all* deals in a given location. You can choose your interests, and they have everything from clothing to wine to food, so it is great across the board. However, the furniture deals can't be beat. You select a category of interest, and then select brands within that interest. The site even breaks the brands into more categories like "trendy." It couldn't be easier to save.

Chapter 6: How to Save on Your Most Important Want: Wardrobe

Everyone likes to look good. In some way, looking good is feeling good. It is way too easy to spend money on looking good. Clothing and accessories are expensive. According to a recent article in InStyle magazine, the average American spends $1,700 every year on clothing and accessories. That is how much money I spent to take a trip to Amsterdam, just to put it in perspective.

So how can you look good and feel good, and perhaps still take a trip to Amsterdam? There are a few ways you can start. The key to savvy shopping really has less to do with deals and sales than it does with staying sharp. As with most money saving techniques, you have to take a little extra time, make lists, and think twice. All in all, it's not that hard. And do not worry: you can still splurge on something great every once in awhile.

Step One: De-Cluttering

When I was a kid, my favorite time of year was "back to school shopping"—that last few weeks of summer where everyone was buying clothes and shoes for the new school year. My least favorite time of year was the week right before "back to school shopping," because that was the week that my mom made me go through every article of clothing I owned and decide to "keep" or "toss." I dreaded this activity so much that I once offered to pay my younger brother to do it for me.

It is something I still dread, even as an adult. Unfortunately it's a very important part of being a savvy shopper. Letting the clothing pile up without ever "tossing" anything is dangerous. You don't *really* know what's in your closet. You end up buying repeat items. Not to mention you can't close the door, and it takes hours to get ready every day. Let us not underestimate minimalism. If you know what works, that's all you need.

There are two ways to do this. One takes six months, and one takes one day. The end result of both is less in your closet and drawers. I recommend the faster method—it's like ripping off a band-aid—easier to get it over with.

First method:
1. Take everything out of your closet.
2. Put everything back in your closet, with the hangers hooked on the wrong way.
3. In 6 months, anything that you haven't worn will be on a hanger that is hooked backwards.
4. "Toss" all of the things that are on backwards hangers.

5. Take a look at all of the items that you are getting rid of: are there any similarities? Maybe they are all florals? Short skirts? Remember any patterns.
6. Enjoy a less cluttered closet.

Second method:
1. Get three boxes (any boxes you can find will work just fine).
2. Label the boxes "keep" "toss" and "maybe".
3. Take everything out of your closet.
4. Sort through your clothing and decide what you are going to keep. These should be items that you wear often enough for others in your life to recognize them ("Oh, that green shirt you have! I love that one.") and things that you have worn more than once in the last six months. Put these items in the "keep" box.
5. Sort through your remaining clothing and decide what you are going to "toss." These should be things you haven't worn in six months to one year (one year for seasonal items). This box often also includes anything gifted to you by your grandmother. Take a look at your "toss" box—see any patterns? Remember them!
6. The remaining clothes are your "maybe" pile. At this point, I usually like to go through them again and see if I can sort

them neatly into either "keep" or "toss." That is not mandatory.
7. Take your "maybe" box, close it, and put it in your closet somewhere.
8. In six months, if you haven't gone into the "maybe" box to fish out some cute top that is perfect, get rid of your "maybes:" they were "toss" material all along, and you were just being sentimental.
9. Enjoy a de-cluttered closet.

I recently read a tip from Gretchen Rubin in her book, *The Happiness Project*. She recommends keeping one shelf in your closet completely empty. Empty it, and don't buy more things to fill it up. For her, this is not a trick to save money; it is merely a component of her happiness to have an empty shelf. I think it is a great idea—challenge yourself to keep that shelf empty, and you will have fewer things. Have fewer things, and you will spend less money.

In order to have fewer things, you must deal with your "toss" pile immediately. There are dozens of ways to do so. Offer items to your friends and family members. Sell your clothes to a consignment shop—there are many types of these, but I recommend looking into Plato's Closet (platoscloset.com). You can also donate your old clothes to Goodwill or a similar organization.

Step Two: Identifying Your Style Basics

Once you have sorted through your existing wardrobe, it is easy to see what you wear regularly. That is the base of your style. At the same time, it is easy to fall prey to the gods of style and accessorizing and buy things that fall outside of that base.

Magazines are shiny and colorful for a reason: to suck you in and make you want to buy beautiful things. There are several problems with this. The first is that you may be inclined to buy clothing or accessories that you wouldn't normally buy. There's nothing wrong with changing your style, but often these items wind up in the back of your closet with the tags still on them, waiting for another day.

A friend of mine is a great example. Last year she told me, "I want to accessorize better." She spent more than $100 buying tons of great necklaces and belts and even a stand to hang her necklaces on. She wears the same necklace every single day. She had that necklace before she went on this shopping spree. The trick is to know *you* better than the shiny magazines do. I know, for example, that I shouldn't wear mustard yellow. Last week I saw a "style guide" in InStyle that said *anyone* could wear mustard yellow if they mix and match it with the right other colors. Wrong.

When I look in my newly de-cluttered

closet, I see a few general categories of clothing items. These categories, luckily, fit neatly with the type of clothing I have to wear to work. Generally, people spend 40 hours of their week working. That means that buying a lot of clothing you can't wear to work is a very silly thing to do. I was happy to see that my closet was full of blazers, button downs, work-friendly blouses, and dresses. If I had lots of glittery, gauzy tank tops and sequin dresses, I would have been a little worried. Those are things you definitely can't wear in my office, and I do not spend much time in nightclubs.

To identify your style basics, think about the following:

- What colors look best on you? What colors do you have most of in your closet?
- What type of clothing do you have to wear to work? Business casual? Business professional? Casual? Athletic?
- What type of clothing suits your body type? Are you better in knee-length, below the knee? Does a cowl neck suit you, or does a v-neck look better?
- What materials do you feel most comfortable in? Silky blend blouses? Wool and cotton?

The point of these questions is to help

keep you from buying something just because it looks pretty. It could look beautiful on a mannequin, your roommate, your sister, your boss—but if it's not for you, you're not going to wear it. That is money wasted, and no trip to Amsterdam.

Step Three: Think "Outfits"

Once you've identified your style basics, you will know where there are gaps in your wardrobe. These gaps are what you should be filling when you go shopping. For example, I have quite a big collection of blazers. Usually I just wear simple tanks or blouses under them. After de-cluttering my closet, I noticed that I don't have a simple white blouse that looks good under a blazer. This gap is why I will go to the mall, and it will help to keep me on track. I don't need anything else—just a cute, white top.

When that gap is filled, I can easily make an outfit or two with it. This is something that is crucial when it comes to saving money on clothes: think in terms of outfits more than items. We don't wear just one piece of clothing at a time, so why would we choose to buy an item of clothing in a vacuum, without considering what outfits can be made from it? That is, when looking at an item of clothing, ask yourself what outfits you can work it into.

It helps if you have a few simple, "go-to"

type outfits in your mind. It also helps on days when you're running late. Put together a few basics in your mind and you'll save yourself time and hopefully money too, if you're doing it right.

Identifying these "go-to" outfits also helps you to notice when an item of clothing is starting to wear out. A few of my "go-to" outfits require more form-fitting button down shirts. One of these shirts is starting to fade a bit now that I have had it for awhile. It is navy blue, so unfortunately the fade is getting obvious. It's time to get a new one. The need for replacements is another reason I will go to the mall.

So right there, I have two reasons to go to the mall: I need a cute, white blouse to build a couple outfits with. I need a new blue button down to replace the one that is getting a bit too old to wear. Notice that neither of these reasons are "because I need to go shopping" or "I just want to look." Falling into those traps is a sure way to spend money that you didn't budget for or plan to spend.

Think outfits, not items. Let this be your mantra about both your closet itself and about your shopping habits. Of course, it is always fun to try new things, and I am not recommending that we all wear the same three outfits from now until death. With 10 items, though, if they are basic and comfortable, and you know that they work for you, you can make at least 20 different outfits. Trying a new style (Preppy? Bohemian?

Sure!) is a great reason to borrow something from your sister, friend, mother, co-worker. I learned that I still couldn't wear mustard yellow because I borrowed a blouse from my sister for one day, not because I bought one.

Where to Shop and Save

Most people shop in malls for things like clothes and accessories. I certainly do. Sadly, once you're inside the mall, it's much easier to spend money! That is why I recommended going in with a plan in earlier sections. However, when I can, I also try to avoid the mall. There are places to shop that are not attached to a food court.

First, try shopping in your living room. By that I mean, invite all of your friends over for a "swap" party. These have been wildly successful for me in the past. Make a little event out of it, and it will be even more successful. Make some food (try a recipe from BudgetBytes!) and ask your friends to bring wine (or whatever they prefer). Ask everyone to bring 7-10 items that they no longer want. Ideally, these items will be a relatively even mix of clothing and accessories. When your friends arrive with their stuff, lay everything out—on tables, couches, chairs—and start shopping. Your clothes get a new life with someone you care about, so you can always borrow them back if you really need to. Plus you get to add interesting new pieces to your wardrobe without spending any money on clothing.

Consignment shops are another great option for cheap, great finds. Really, any of the places listed above where you can donate clothing (or sell your clothing) are great spots to pick up something "new" and interesting. It's also possible to find something great and trendy at a place like Goodwill. For example, last summer, when the trend of long, flowing maxi dresses was in full swing, I found one at Goodwill for $12.50. There's nothing about Goodwill clothing that a run through my washing machine and a little fabric softener can't fix. It gets donated every day by people just like you and me.

Instead of hitting the mall, you should also look at places like T.J. Maxx, Kohl's and Marshalls. These one-stop shopping super stores really do have what they advertise: lots of great, name brand, good quality clothing for lower prices than you will find in any mall. Kohl's specifically has great deals—they send out weekly coupons, sometimes up to 50%. At the end of the quarter, you get Kohl's cash back that you can spend on anything in the store. I once bought a sweater from Kohl's that was originally priced for $50. I got it for $12. It was not luck of the draw—I registered online at Kohls.com (you can also do this through the cashier by giving your e-mail address) and simply pulled up coupons and Kohl's cash through e-mail on my smart phone. Instant savings!

Finally, if you are a shopping mall enthusiast, there are ways to save even there. First, make a list of the stores you shop at most regularly. Look into the top three stores you shop in. Most stores offer credit cards with some kind of rewards program. If you really love a particular store (and only if you *really* love it) it may be worthwhile to check out the rewards or credit card program that store offers. Take, for example, Banana Republic (which is connected to Gap, Piperlime, Old Navy, and Athleta as well). Signing up for a Banana Republic credit card automatically gives you $10.00 reward card back for every $200.00 you spend in store or online. You also earn "points" using this card—and $1 spent on your Banana Republic card earns 1 point. When you get to 1,000 points, you get a $10.00 reward card.

The card also gives you other rewards. You get the advance notice of sales, promotions and discounts e-mailed to you. You get birthday rewards. You also get 10% off at Gap, Old Navy, and Piperlime on Tuesdays.

The Bottom Line

There are simple ways to avoid spending a lot of money on clothing. They do not require many big life changes or even signing up for rewards programs. Here are some simple tricks that your mother probably told you:

- Don't be lured by sales.
- Go into every store or shopping mall with a plan of action.
- If you can, use cash (use this tip to save money on everything, forever, because it makes you accountable).
- Shop out of season for big ticket items like coats and bathing suits.
- Look for online deals.

Some of these simple tips are not always possible (I rarely shop using only cash, for example), but some are great. There are tons of ways to look for online deals, for example.

Let Your Technology Help You Save on Clothes and Accessories

Nowadays, there is an entire world of clothes shopping online. There are e-mail subscriptions that send updates about sales on designer goods. There are sites that allow you to get updates from just the stores you love when an online sale is happening. Store websites are not always very user-friendly. I usually have to look a little before I find sale items. Notably, most websites do not have a section for "clearance" items as the store would. The clearance items are there, however—just type "clearance" into the search bar on the webpage. These items are usually about 20% cheaper than just the sale items.

Here are some ways that you can make the World Wide Web work for you:

- GILT.com
  This website allows you to sign up for daily e-mails about sales. They are not just any sales, however—they are designer sales, with a certain number of sizes and styles. When those run out, you may be able to get on a waiting list, but chances are you're out of luck. There are usually about five to ten different sales per category, and the categories include the standard: men's, women's, kids', and home. For example, in the women's section, generally there's a sale for jewelry, specific types or brands of clothing, scarves, purses, etc. The sales begin every day at 12 Noon EST. There are several other websites that do this, and they include RueLaLa.com, HauteLook.com, and

BeyondtheRack.com—and they are all free to sign up. The deals on all of these sites are advertised as "up to 80% off designer goods" and as a GILT convert myself, I can say with confidence that it is worth it to get the e-mails every day!

- Dealnews.com
  This website has coupon codes for various stores. They can only be used online, but they are sometimes up to 75% off at great stores like Banana Republic, for example. This site is great mostly because it pulls a bunch of information together onto one site.

- Shopittome.com
  This is a great site if you want to know only about specific retailers, and you don't want to get ten e-mails per day. This site lets you select which retailers you are interested in when you register and will send you email updates only about the deals that you are interested in.

- ShopStyle mobile app
  This app allows you to compare prices of more than 300 retailers across different categories, including men, women, kids, and even home furnishings. You can sort by any category—price, color, brand

name. It's great, and it's right on your phone.

- TouchCloset
    This app is $.99, but if you want to track your closet in a more organized way and make the pieces you already have work for you, this is very helpful. The app allows you to catalog all of your clothing. You can plan outfits on the go. Instead of buying new clothing, this app makes it really easy for you to work with what you've already got, which saves you even more.

- Love it Or Lose it
    This app is perfect for the days when you have wandered into the mall alone and are about to spend a bunch of money. Download this app for $.99, then upload a picture of whatever item you are about to buy. You will get instant feedback from "fashionistas" all over the world who also have the app. You will know almost immediately if the item is worth buying. It's like having dozens of second opinions and can keep you from buying that oversized magenta sweater you would have bought if no one talked you out of it.

Chapter 7: Save on Entertainment and Lifestyle—Live a Full Life on a Budget

Watch Movies on the Cheap

There are some fairly obvious ways to start saving money when you want to go to the movies. The first is to see an earlier movie—matinee or even morning movies on the weekends are usually at least $4.00 to $5.00 cheaper. You can also shop around—maybe the 12-screen IMAX theater up the block is your favorite, but look for dollar theaters near you. Use a site like moviefone.com to search, because this site lists dollar theaters along with all the others.

You can also save at the movie theater by only going to the theater on a discount or bargain day. My movie theater has "bargain Tuesday" where all movies are $5. Though I'd prefer date night to be on a Friday, it's nice to save money and see a current movie on a big screen. Plus, date night on Tuesdays is a nice way to break up your work week.

When you go to a movie, eat first. You won't be tempted to spend a ridiculous amount of money on popcorn and soft drinks. Give yourself enough time to plan a meal or at least a snack beforehand. The markup on snacks is bad on your wallet, and the snacks themselves are bad for your body.

Joining your movie theater's rewards program is a great way to keep a bit of money in your pocket. This is more worthwhile if you see a lot of movies, but it can help over time even if you just go a few times a year. For example, let's take a look at Regal Crown Club. This is a rewards program in which you sign up for a free card. You present that card every time you see a movie at a Regal theater, and you gain points for every ticket you buy. These points add up and you can use them on anything at the theater, from tickets to popcorn. Regal Crown Club gives you 1 point for every $1.00 you spend. You can earn up to 20 points per day. When you accumulate 50 points, you get one free small popcorn … and so on, and so on, for more points.

Finally, if you know that you are an avid movie-goer, there is no reason that you can't simply buy tickets in bulk. Most large or chain movie theaters offer discounted tickets—you just have to buy a lot of them. These tickets do not work with special movies, like IMAX or 3D. I'd recommend not seeing those types of movies anyway, if you're trying to save money, as they are much more expensive. If you really want to see a movie in 3D, check out the website RealorFake3D.com. It will tell you a bit about whether or not the movie is really 3D, or just retrofitted. It sometimes also says a bit about the quality you can expect, so you're less likely to wind up wasting money on a 3D movie that you didn't need to see in 3D.

Watch Movies for Even Cheaper—At Home

Although it does require a bit of a sacrifice if you are a lover of watching movies on a big screen, you can save a lot more money if you watch movies at home. There are many ways to do this, and your level of commitment can make the home-movie experience really worthwhile, if you're willing.

First, think about starting a DVD swap with your friends, family members, or co-workers. In my office, we have a monthly DVD swap. It's not very organized, but once a month people bring in DVDs and other people bring them home. They usually reappear in the office just in time for the next DVD swap. It's a great way to watch movies for free. As an added bonus, in an office, everyone has different taste in movies. This results in a much bigger variety to choose from.

Join Netflix. It is under $10.00 a month for unlimited streaming of TV shows and movies. Yes, not everything is instantly streamable on your computer. Those movies can easily be put on your DVD "queue" and mailed to you, if you bump up your membership level just a bit.

Netflix and other similar streaming sites are revolutionizing the entertainment industry. Don't miss the boat! Join now and get your first month for free at Netflix.com.

Hulu.com is a website that streams TV shows and movies, too. It's free at its basic level. It has shows like Saturday Night Live and Modern Family, so the shows are not outdated just because they are offered for free. The downside to Hulu, of course, is advertisements—but commercials have been on TV for years, right? Joining HuluPlus, their paid membership, gives you unlimited streaming for just $7.99 every month.

Amazon Prime is my personal favorite way to watch movies on the cheap. Amazon Prime is a special membership through Amazon for $79.00 per year. Prime gives you lots of benefits aside from movies (including free shipping and special deals just for Prime members). Most importantly, it gives you access to a selection of the movies and TV shows on Amazon's database instantly. It's common knowledge that amazon.com has *everything*, so it is natural to understand that they have *so many movies*. I am never bored.

Perhaps a Prime membership is not for you, but you're already paying for cable. If you're already paying for cable packages with On Demand, check out your On Demand first. My cable provider has a "same day as theaters" option where you can buy a movie for $6.99. There are also hundreds of free movies on demand for you to watch instantly on your TV. Why not utilize a service you're already paying for before thinking about paying for another one?

Another great way to save on movies is one that works for just about anybody. Find a RedBox. This literally red box can be found in grocery stores and drugs stores all over. It allows you to rent a movie for just over $1.00. You can do so with your debit or credit card. Just remember to return them quickly! You can find a RedBox near you at redbox.com/locations. According to their website, there are at least 200 movies in each box. They also offer video games!

Finally, check your local library. As so much of life has gone Wi-Fi, we tend to forget about the library. Library cards are free. Most libraries have movies to check out. My library even has a new releases section, so the movies are fairly up to date. Just be careful about returning them on time—the fee for a late movie at the library is generally higher than the fee for a late book.

Staying Fit Without Breaking the Bank

So, you want to stay in shape, but you can't afford a gym membership. Don't worry, there are ways for you to stay fit without spending too much. There are ways to stay in shape that are free, of course, so I'll start with those.

The first way to stay fit for free is to get outside. Run. Walk. Power walk. Play basketball in a park. All of these are free, given that you have a pair of sneakers lying around. If you don't, look for a pair on one of the great websites listed in the wardrobe section! Everyone needs a pair of sneakers.

Another free way to lose weight is to check out the workout videos on Hulu.com. There is an entire section on Hulu.com dedicated to yoga and Pilates classes, as well as a few kickboxing videos. They are very informative, and the video quality is great. All you need is some open space in your living room.

If you'd prefer to attend a class or a gym, first look into any discount or "cheap" gyms in your area. Most "fancier" gyms have a membership fee per month, plus an enrollment fee. Some of the "budget" gyms—Planet Fitness and LA Fitness—will waive the enrollment fee and charge only $10 or $20 per month. Beware, however—many, many people I have spoken with said that they regret their gym membership, because it is a money drain. Often, we are too busy to get to the gym more than once a week. This means you are paying for a service that you are not using, and that is the opposite of saving money.

You can also take a look at one of the "fancier" gyms. Talk to someone at every gym in your area. Most of these gyms have "membership specialists." Their entire job is to sell memberships to their gym. They often do this by offering free classes (not dozens, but a few), a free facility tour, or a free consultation with a trainer. This is a great way to get a feel for different gyms, first to see *what* is really worth the hefty price tag, and second, to get in a free class or two if you don't plan on buying a membership.

Yoga and Pilates studios often do the same thing that gyms do. Because these classes are more specialized and come in many different styles, most studios offer a free class for new students. Some really great yoga studios, like Core Power Yoga (corepoweryoga.com) offer a free week of classes. At most private studios, if the prices are way out of your budget, you can offer to clean the studio after class to get discounted or even free classes.

Finally, look into all the benefits of your health insurance plans. Some plans offer reimbursement for your gym membership up to a certain dollar amount. Some plans cover a certain number of yoga classes. It never hurts to ask—look into your package now. My health insurance plan will cover up to $200 per 6-month period for either yoga or a gym membership. The downside is that you have to pay out of pocket first, but the reimbursement is great.

You can stay healthy and fit without spending hundreds of dollars every month despite the fact that there are tons of gyms charging that much. If running is not for you, try stopping at a local gym for a free class—get at least a little exercise, for free!

Chapter 8: Anyone Can Live on a Budget

If I Can, You Can

It is difficult to save money. That is no secret. The key is to commit to doing it, at least in small ways. Many people get discouraged because they aren't saving tons of money every month, like my sister, who gets upset that she is not able to put hundreds in her savings account out of every paycheck. What must be understood, though, is that most people are not able to save money that way.

Saving money in small, everyday ways makes it more manageable. In the first month of your money saving journey, simply look at your bottom line at the end of every month. Do you have a little bit more than you usually do? If so, you're making progress.

I started saving money incrementally, without making any huge lifestyle changes. I still go out for drinks or dinner. I just don't do it every night (and usually not twice in the same week). I still get spa-level pampering. I just do it once a month or less, instead of weekly. I still feel good and look good in great clothes. I just paid less for them or, better yet, learned how to re-vamp them to make them even cuter.

All of these little ways I started saving money began with a little extra thought and planning. It takes time to stick to a budget. It takes willpower to say "no thanks" to the third margarita night of the week. It's easier with a plan, because a plan holds you a bit more accountable for your spending. Plan a bit first, and keep track of what you spend as you go. You will not only be completely in control of your money but, more importantly, you will be able to notice the areas where you are saving—that's something to get excited about.

What is Saving Money All About

Saving money is different for every person. Identifying why you want to (or need to) start saving money is the most important step in the process. If you arbitrarily decide to make a budget, it may not work for you. If there is no rationale behind your frugality besides "it's smart to save," your saving probably won't be very successful. "Smart" is a concept—it's smart to save money. There is nothing tangible behind it. Think about it. There are many things that are "smart" to do that people have trouble doing. Quitting smoking is smart, but it's hard to do. Eating healthy is smart, but it's hard to do.

These things, saving money included, are smart to do, but there are many things distracting us from doing them every day. Establishing a stable motivation behind something is a sure fire way to accomplish it. Save money for a purpose—whatever that is—and you will be successful. Otherwise, what is to justify *not* spending that money on a new handbag? If you're not putting your money away *for a reason*, there is no justification for not buying that thing you want. Except, of course, that it's smarter not to. However, that is not very realistic.

Find your motivation and remind yourself of it as often as you can. Yes, saving money is smart—but only if you can do it successfully. If you can't, it's frustrating, demeaning, and stressful.

Savings Summary: Key Tips to Remember

1. Find your motivation to save: saving money because it's "smart" is abstract. It doesn't connect you with anything solid to make you want to save money, even when it is really difficult. Thinking about what you would put all of your saved money toward *before* you write your budget is a great way to set goals and expectations for yourself from the start.

2. Make a plan for savings: establish where you are spending the most money, and try to cut back in those areas. Websites like

mint.com can help you do this. To stay on a budget, you must first *make* a budget.

3. Keep track of the money you spend: with debit cards it is too easy to swipe and forget. Keep receipts. Put them all in one place. If keeping paper is not for you, check your bank account online *constantly.* Not every minute, of course, but set up a routine at least weekly. When you look at your bank account, you should be able to account for every purchase. If you look at it and think "Hum... Where did that come from?" you are probably doing this wrong. A big part of successful saving is holding yourself accountable!

4. Think before you go. If you like eating out, don't just eat at any restaurant, eat at one that you have discovered deals at. Use groupon.com or livingsocial.com to purchase deals like "$25 to spend on food and non-alcoholic drinks at a restaurant for only $10." Join restaurant rewards at any restaurant that you frequent. You never know when you may get a free appetizer. Further, *fill out survey cards!* Filling out the survey (either online or on a card they bring with your check) can sometimes get you rewards. My favorite

local restaurant has an online survey. If you give the waitress your completion code, you get a free appetizer. The best news? There is no limit to how many times you can do this!

5. Think before you buy. Make a plan of your meals for the week. Take a little extra time to think (at least) about the basic food groups you want to eat or serve. Then hit the coupons, or couponing apps. There is almost never a reason to pay full price for every single grocery item. You end up spending more money on groceries when you decide last minute that you need something, and you run out to get it. You can also save money by buying local fresh produce. Better yet, you can start your own garden and never pay for veggies again.

6. Turn off your lights! Change your light bulbs to ones that use less energy. Be aware that a lot of energy is spent *heating water*! Wash your clothes on cold unless they're filthy, take shorter or colder showers, and run your dishwasher only when it is full. Pay attention to your appliances and what settings they have and make them work a bit harder for you to save some money on bills every

month!

7. Spend a little extra time before you hop in the car to save money on gas. Look at websites like gasbuddy.com to get the cheapest gas in your area. Before you hop in the car to go on vacation, calculate your mileage and the cost of gas using gasbuddy.com. Seeing the cost of that travel may—should!—encourage you to look into budget traveling options like Megabus. You can even go to Canada with Megabus!

8. Clothing is one of the biggest expenses in my budget. It's usually the biggest expense in most other people's budgets too. Sign up for rewards cards or credit cards at your favorite stores to get points and money back for what you spend. Stay away from shopping malls and sales that get you in the door to "save"—these can result in you spending money on things you were never planning to buy. De-clutter your closet (and your life!) in order to determine what clothing you actually need to buy, what clothing you already have, and what clothing looks best on you. You can save a lot of money when you are clothes shopping if you buy either *items you need* or *items you can*

easily build into existing outfits. As a general rule, try to buy only those items! Buying the latest trend won't make you trendy if you never wear it—think of my friend and all of her new necklaces, still hanging and never worn.

9. Saving on entertainment is not impossible, though it may take some sacrifice. I'm not saying that you should never go to the movies again. However, you should realize that movies are a bit of a "rip off" and try to avoid paying full price at all costs. Matinees and rewards programs help you save money in the theater, and eating before you go keeps you from splurging (not to mention binging!) on popcorn and soda while you're there. Look into any of the great ways in this book to watch movies at home—either for free, or for very little. For example, sign up for Netflix or check your local library, and you'll be watching movies and television shows in no time— within your budget.

10. Let the internet work for you. Use technology to your advantage. If you know that you need to buy something, don't just head to the store. Check online first, and see if there are any deals. If you

already do a lot of online shopping, I recommend using freeshipping.org, which, just like it sounds, offers free shipping. Look through your smart phone for free apps related to deals of all kinds. There are hundreds of new phone apps made every single day. Tons of these apps are about ways to make our lives easier. What better way to make life easier than to make saving money easier? Search now and save.

Good Luck! Now Go Start Saving

The bottom line is: anyone can save. All you need to do is stop and think. Think about what you need. Think less about what you *want.* Write down what you need and look for the best deals before you buy those things. Stick only to the things you write down. If you stray from your list, make sure it's for something you will use and that it is within your budget.

You don't have to give up anything in your life in order to save money, except time for thinking and planning. You may need to cut back in some areas—like entertainment or eating in restaurants—but you don't have to give up anything completely. Living frugally doesn't have to be an exercise in futility, especially if you let technology help you along the way.

Wrapping Up: List of Sites and Apps Mentioned

General Budgeting and Keeping Track of Finances:
1. Mint.com
2. Rudder.com
3. Geezeo.com

Eating:
1. Restaurants.com
2. Groupon.com
3. Scoutmob - mobile application
4. ChowHound.com
5. CouponSherpa - mobile application and website
6. GroceryIQ - mobile application and website
7. Coupons.com

Utilities:
1. Billshrink.com

Girly Goods and Services:
1. CVS.com
2. Groupon.com
3. LivingSocial.com

Transportation:
1. Fueleconomy.gov

2. Gasbuddy.com
3. Wikihow.com/save-money-on-gas
4. Edmunds.com

Home Décor:
1. Onekingslane.com
2. DealDecor.com
3. YipIt.com

Shopping:
1. GILT.com
2. RueLaLa.com
3. HauteLook.com
4. BeyondtheRack.com
5. Dealnews.com
6. Shopittome.com
7. ShopStyle - mobile application
8. TouchCloset - mobile application
9. Love it Or Lose it - mobile application

Entertainment:
1. Netflix.com
2. Hulu.com
3. Redbox.com

**Visit
EmpowermentNation.com
to view other fantastic books and to
sign up for book alerts, giveaways,
and updates!**

www.ingramcontent.com/pod-product-compliance
Lightning Source LLC
Chambersburg PA
CBHW071801200526
45167CB00017B/993